I0879153

WESTBURY

FROM ABOVE

Holy Rood Cemetery.

WESTBURY
FROM ABOVE

RICHARD PANCHYK

AMERICA THROUGH TIME®
ADDING COLOR TO AMERICAN HISTORY

America Through Time is an imprint of Fonthill Media LLC
www.through-time.com
office@through-time.com

Published by Arcadia Publishing by arrangement with Fonthill Media LLC
For all general information, please contact Arcadia Publishing:
Telephone: 843-853-2070
Fax: 843-853-0044
E-mail: sales@arcadiapublishing.com
For customer service and orders:
Toll-Free 1-888-313-2665

www.arcadiapublishing.com

First published 2019

Copyright © Richard Panchyk 2019

ISBN 978-1-63499-159-9

All rights reserved. No part of this publication may be reproduced, stored in a retrieval system or transmitted in any form or by any means, electronic, mechanical, photocopying, recording or otherwise, without prior permission in writing from Fonthill Media LLC

Typeset in Mrs Eaves XL Serif Narrow
Printed and bound in England

Acknowledgments

Thanks to Alan Sutton for developing this series, and thanks to Kena Longabaugh and Jamie Sutton for getting the manuscript ready for publication. Thanks to Susan Kovarik and the Historical Society of the Westburys for the use of many wonderful historic images. Also thanks to Matthew and Elizabeth for their assistance.

All photos are courtesy of the author except for pages 13 bottom, 14 top, 18 top, 22 bottom, 27, 28, 29 top, 34, 41 top, 42 top, 43 bottom, 50 bottom, 55 top, 56 bottom, 59, 61, 64, 66 top, 69 bottom, 70 bottom, 75 top, 77, 88 bottom, and 92, courtesy of the Historical Society of the Westburys; and 88 top courtesy of the National Archives.

Northern Westbury.

Introduction

Westbury from Above is part of a new book series that strives to capture history from a new angle, one that is seldom seen in the thousands of local history books currently on the market. It is appropriate that Westbury is the first book in this series, given its place in aviation history; the spot where Charles Lindbergh's plane became airborne on its famous transatlantic voyage is in Westbury.

The concept of the bird's-eye view dates back centuries, but was most popular in the nineteenth century and was a great way to depict the great growth of the many villages, towns, and cities across the United States. No street-level view can capture the essence of a neighborhood the way a bird's-eye view can—literally called that because only birds could see such sights in those days, as people had not yet gained the ability to fly. With the advent of airplanes, aerial views were now possible, but most of these were taken from heights well over 1,000 feet. Drone technology has made possible the capturing of views from lesser altitudes, where more detail can be captured and a greater sense of place can be established. What began as simply a fun way to see my town from a new perspective eventually turned into an idea to create something to share with other history enthusiasts. Looking at the photos in this book has a twofold benefit: seeing Westbury from above for the first time, but more importantly, offering a better understanding of how today's landscape was shaped by yesterday's history.

Whether you already know a great deal about Westbury's history or are just dipping your toes in for the first time now, this book offers a new take, a different perspective. The photos in this book represent many different geographical areas and thus different parts of Westbury's long and fascinating history. These views from above are supplemented by historical photographs to help document Westbury's rich heritage.

First settled in the mid-seventeenth century, Westbury was named after a village in the Wiltshire region of England, from whence one of its founders, Henry Willis, came. Westbury's early existence was a quiet, peaceful one. Located at the northern edge of the Hempstead Plains, once the greatest expanse of grassland east of the Mississippi, Westbury was, from the start, in a prime location. There was good, flat farmland, but also the beginnings of hills and woodlands to the north. Centrally located, Westbury was one of the early stops on the nascent Long Island Rail Road in the mid-nineteenth century.

The Westbury Quakers built a meetinghouse in 1702, at what is now the intersection of Post Avenue and Jericho Turnpike. Around the same time, they also founded a cemetery on the property. A walk through the cemetery today is like a lesson in both Westbury history and local Quaker history. Many of the names on the gravestones were founding families in the early years of the community, and the nearby vicinity—Post, Hicks, Willis, Albertson, and Carle, to name a few. Though many of the earliest stones are sunken and the lettering faded, there are still some legible eighteenth- and early-nineteenth-century stones to be found. Westbury's Quakers were forward thinking and in 1775 they freed all 154 of their African-American slaves, many of whom went on to raise their families in the Westbury area and become an important part of the story of the community's growth.

Westbury's sleepy existence did change with the coming of the railroad and the influx of Irish and German immigrants in the mid-nineteenth century (followed by Italians later on). St. Brigid's Church was built in 1854 to cater to the rising number of Catholics in the area; just decades earlier there had been only a handful nearby, but the numbers were growing quickly. The village proper was also growing, centered near the rail station and to the north along Post Avenue. The early schools were located to the north, on or near what is now Jefferson Street. Westbury High School is actually in Old Westbury, on one-time Quaker land that was more recently part of the Howard Phipps estate (Howard was the brother of Jay Phipps, whose home and estate became Old Westbury Gardens). At the turn of the twentieth century, Quaker Westbury north of the village still had a pastoral, old-time feel. A short note from *circa* 1900—found among some papers stuffed inside a wood burning stove during an estate sale years ago in an old Quaker house on the north side of Jericho Turnpike—gives a feel for the old Quaker days: "I have been here over an hour and have had a very pleasant time with thee. I hope to come often, and shall be glad to have thee come to see me, and I hope we can have more rides later. I must say good bye." Another little note reads: "I am glad they so much enjoyed their trip, and were not sick. Carrie Sharpliss will be quite a traveler soon, she has been on many trips already. Will thy little boy Paul go with thee, or remain with his grandmother? I saw Mariana and Carrie pass with a team of horses."

Things were about to change for the Quakers, however. By the turn of the twentieth century, the first wealthy Manhattanites had begun building their large Gold Coast estates in the northern part of the newly created Nassau County. These vast estates extended as far south as Westbury (the section that is now Old Westbury), and much land was purchased from Quakers, including the property that is now Old Westbury Gardens. There was a growing need for construction labor, because of the sheer size of these palatial homes and all their outbuildings—as well as all the physical moving of earth and planting of gardens that needed to take place. It was not convenient nor cost effective for these workers to commute from great distances, so many of them wound up settling in Westbury and other nearby communities.

But construction of these large mansions and landscaped grounds was not the end of the work. Once the estates were built, it would take a large staff of workers to service each estate and keep it running smoothly, anywhere from ten to dozens of people per estate. Butlers, maids, cooks, nannies, nurses, chauffeurs, stable hands, groomers, and gardeners were all needed. Besides these full-time workers, there were of course all the others needed to do occasional handywork and repairs, including plumbers, electricians, roofers, and carpenters. And there was a need for specialty supplies—especially horse-related equipment, since many of these estates had horses and their owners were active polo players. The Gold Coast was a big business for Westbury, which was very conveniently located to serve the estates. A look at the census of 1920 reveals that half of the heads of household in Westbury had an occupation that was related to serving the estates. That's an incredible number, and a testament to the fact that Westbury's biggest growth did not come, like some other Long Island communities, as a suburb to New York City—it grew on its own strength fueled by the local economy. Westbury was a suburb of the nearby Gold Coast.

One reminder within Westbury of its Gold Coast heritage is the Episcopal Church of the Advent on Jericho Turnpike. It was designed by famous architect John Russell Pope (who designed the Jefferson Memorial and the Lincoln Birthplace Memorial in Kentucky) and built in 1910 specifically to serve the needs of some of the Gold Coast residents, and was the scene of several high-society weddings.

Throughout all the changes, the Quaker presence remained strong. The old Quaker meetinghouse burned down and was replaced with the current one in 1902. Another building on the Quaker property dates to *circa* 1840. Since 1957, the property has also been home to the Westbury Friends School. The cemetery continues to bury members of local Quaker families to this day.

Westbury is home to one of Long Island's oldest businesses: the popular Hicks Nurseries was founded in 1853, supplying plants and flowers to the area well before the advent of the Gold Coast. Once the estates were being built, Hicks quickly adapted to this new market and became the go-to supplier for trees and shrubs for the gardens and lawns of a great many Gold Coast mansions. Their popularity was due in part to their personal service—they not only sold trees, they delivered and planted them and offered advice and extensive knowledge. Hicks' advertisements of the time showed their focus on estates—a 1906 advertisement said Hicks could offer evergreens by the 100,000s. A 1909 advertisement proclaimed that Hicks had 1,000 big trees up to 28 feet tall that were ready to be planted. The ads asked estate owners the pointed question: why should they have to wait twenty-five years for a tree to grow when they could buy them now already grown? The trees could be shipped up to 1,500 miles.

Meanwhile, the next wave of immigrants had arrived in the late nineteenth and early twentieth century, from Italy. In fact, many Italian immigrant families to Westbury came from a specific community—Durazzano, about 20 miles north of Naples. St. Brigid's outgrew its old church and in 1894 a new one was built. Within just twenty years, the growing community outgrew that church as well and the current stone church was completed in 1916. Its predecessor was moved across the street and serves as the parish hall. Westbury's diversity is reflected in the variety of churches that have been built over the years.

As late as 1905, most of the land south of Jericho bordered by Hicks on the west and Post Avenue on the east was farmland, owned by Wilbur Lewis (Lewis Avenue is named after him) and Edmund and William Post. Things changed rapidly in the next decade, with farmland being sold off and homes built. The majority of the homes standing today in the Village of Westbury are colonials that were built between 1905 and 1930, which was the height of the era of the great estates. These were not humble or small abodes by any means; many of the estate workers had steady work and good pay and could afford to build a three- or four-bedroom houses. The village was growing and changing fast. In fact, the Harris family's house, which was where the piazza is now at the intersection of Maple Avenue and Post Avenue, was in a quiet enough location when built, but just a few years later, Mr. Harris (who ran a bicycle shop in town) wanted to get away from the bustle of downtown, so he had the entire house moved about five blocks north to Fulton Street and Wilson Avenue.

Westbury was the site of the nation's first ever train-car collision. The accident occurred at the Post Avenue crossing, which was at grade back then (a bridge was finally built in 1914). In 1901, a French race car driver named Henri Fournier was visiting New York, and had just returned from the Meadowbrook Hunt with some friends, when his car was struck as it headed north across the tracks. Fournier survived but passengers in his car were seriously injured. It's likely that the wealthy William K. Vanderbilt, who was in a car just ahead of the accident, was inspired by this crash when he created the Long Island Motor Parkway a few years later—a grade separated highway with dozens of bridges and no grade crossings of roads or railroads.

Providing support for estates was not twentieth-century Westbury's only claim to fame. Westbury was responsible for rocking the Cradle of Aviation; the growing aviation industry was centered just south of the village proper. Roosevelt Field, first opened in 1917, spanned the south side of Old Country Road from Clinton Avenue all the way to Merchants Concourse. A great moment in Westbury history was when Lindbergh's plane, The Spirit of St. Louis, took off from Roosevelt Field in May of 1927. Lindbergh could be spotted getting an ice cream soda at a Post Avenue drugstore in the days leading up to his historic flight, and on that momentous spring morning in 1927, local residents gathered on Post to watch the plane lift off—there was a clear view down to Old Country Road. The site where Lindbergh's plane became airborne is marked by a small stone monument just south of the Source Mall parking garage.

Westbury also has a place in auto racing history. In 1904, William K. Vanderbilt's Vanderbilt Cup Race was held and the grandstand was located in Westbury, along Jericho Turnpike just east of Post Avenue. A marker near the Church of the Advent notes the site where a huge crowd gathered to watch the racers pass by. In 1936, the Roosevelt Raceway opened south of Old Country Road and was the site of a final Vanderbilt Cup Race. In 1940, the venue was converted into the nation's first track to run harness races. The Raceway was one of the New

York City area's most popular horse racing tracks until changing times and competition from places such as the Meadowlands forced it to close in 1988. Many locals were employed at the track, which had extensive stables on the property. The property was developed as commercial and its name lives on in the AMC Loews Raceway theater on the site.

The Gold Coast estates gradually faded as their owners died and their heirs could not handle the cost or responsibility of maintaining the large properties—and further, after the stock market bust of 1929, many of these estate owners were simply not as wealthy as they had been. But despite the dwindling number of active large estates, Westbury continued to thrive; the former estate workers found plenty of other opportunities as more homes and infrastructure continued to be built—including the Northern State Parkway, which cut through Westbury just south of Hicks Nurseries.

As for Hicks Nurseries, it continued to thrive, but with the demise of the great estates, it did not need as much land as it had amassed, because it was no longer growing as many trees to as mature an age. At its peak, the Hicks Nursery property stretched from Jericho Turnpike all the way to Maple Avenue. Between 1927 and 1939, some of the land was sold off, but the Hicks property was still almost 75 acres and went to Drexel Avenue. Some of the Hicks land south of the current property (south of the parkway) was sold off and homes were built, and the Drexel Avenue School was built on former Hicks property. Nursery Lane and all the tree named streets in the vicinity (Pin Oak, Walnut, Chestnut, Magnolia, etc.) are a tribute to the land's former ownership. Several of the old trees on the Drexel school's property (including a grand old copper beech tree) could date to the Hicks days.

When Roosevelt Field closed in 1950, the land was developed into retail, thus turning the area into one of the most famous shopping malls in the country. For decades, Westbury's biggest retail establishment was the Fortunoff store on Old Country Road (the Roosevelt Field Mall itself is located in Garden City). Opened in 1964, in 1997 the store became the anchor for the Source Mall, which though originally home to more than sixty-five stores and restaurants, failed, and by 2015 was mostly empty. The site was purchased by Lesso Home, which is converting it to a home improvement mall.

In recent years, there has been a growing awareness of Westbury's historical importance. In 2007, my book *A History of Westbury Long Island* was published on the seventy-fifth anniversary of the incorporation of the Village of Westbury. In 2018, several historic markers were placed around the Village to note spots of great importance.

One of the biggest preservation success stories on Long Island has been the rejuvenation of the old 1920s Westbury Theater on Post Avenue. For years an abandoned and crumbling eyesore, the theater was reopened in 2013 as The Space, a performance venue hosting concerts and private events, and has since hosted hundreds of events, including performances by Art Garfunkel, Billy Idol, Steve Winwood, Philip Philips, and many others. The Space was also the site of a historic campaign rally by Hillary Clinton after Hillary's second presidential debate in September 2016. At a 2018 Long Island Music Hall of Fame induction ceremony, Billy Joel appeared at the Space to induct his old friend Elliott Murphy.

Another local success was the removal of a gas station that had long stood on the corner of Post and Maple and its replacement with the Ernesto Strada Piazza. Though the last of the old-time stores vanished when the variety store Tear and Gershon shut down, Post Avenue has seen a revival. The former Tear and Gershon spot, for example, was spruced up and became Café Gino's. Though longtime Post Avenue pizza institution Alfredo's closed in 2017, it was replaced by a new pizzeria. The Village and the rest of Westbury continues to grow and change as the years pass. Government grants and local incentive programs have given many area businesses a facelift, and have rejuvenated or will rejuvenate various areas around Westbury.

Though its auto racing and polo days are gone, Westbury is still a place for recreation. In addition to having several parks and schoolyards of its own, Westbury is just a few minutes from the largest park in Nassau County, Eisenhower Park (which is bigger than Central Park). The late 1990s and early 2000s saw the passing of the last of the old-time Westbury residents who could remember the golden Gold Coast and aviation days of the 1920s and 1930s. Their old houses were sold and new families moved in, and Westbury's story continued to evolve. The legacy of the historic past is ever alive, and it unfolds in the visual story told within the pages of this book.

Note: I have arranged the images in this book roughly from north to south, which actually works well to tell the story of Westbury.

The settlement of Westbury began in the 1660s north of what is now the Northern State Parkway, when Quaker farmers began to settle on land just north of the Hempstead Plains.

Westbury is named after the home of one of its founders: Westbury in Wiltshire, England. Appropriately enough, Westbury, England, is famous for something that is best seen from the air—the 180-foot-high Westbury White Horse, many hundreds of years old and carved into a hill. This image of Westbury probably dates to the 1950s.

One of the most historic locations in Westbury is the Quaker Meeting House on the east side of Post Avenue just south of Jericho Turnpike. The original meetinghouse building on the site dated to 1702, and the current one was built in 1902. This property has been owned by the Quakers for more than 300 years.

The elegant stone Episcopal Church of the Advent is adjacent to the Quaker property. Built in 1910, it catered to the wealthy Gold Coast families who lived north of Jericho Turnpike.

The Quaker cemetery, which is south of the meeting house and other buildings on site, is full of history. The names on the gravestones tell the story of the area's history.

Looking at the southwest corner of the cemetery property, where there is still much available space. The Quaker Cemetery is home to some of the finest evergreen trees in all of Westbury.

OPPOSITE PAGE:

Above: Wandering among the graves, you can find stones dating from the eighteenth century all the way to the present, as the cemetery is still active.

Below: As is evident in this image, some of the Westbury gravestones have sunken into the ground with age. The Westbury Quaker cemetery has a Jericho counterpart that is also historic, though not nearly as sizeable.

The Quakers opened the first school in Westbury during the eighteenth century. This early school building was located near Westbury Pond in what is now Old Westbury.

OPPOSITE PAGE:

Above: Looking north at some of the buildings on the Quaker school campus. Beyond it is Westbury High School, technically located in Old Westbury.

Below: The size of the Quaker meeting house, school, and cemetery property is visible in this image looking north from just south of the Northern State Parkway. The Westbury High School property and the new Catholic cemetery to the north across Jericho Turnpike were both once Quaker-owned farmland, before they were purchased by the Phipps and Hitchcock families, respectively.

Westbury High School is on land that used to be owned by the wealthy Phipps family, who bought it from Quaker families that had owned it previously.

Looking east from the high school grounds. The property at left is "Erchless," the estate that was built by Howard Phipps (younger brother of John S. Phipps, who built Westbury House, aka what is now Old Westbury Gardens) in 1935. Further east is the Catholic Queen of Peace Cemetery under construction.

Looking north toward the Erchless property. Some of the green outbuildings can be seen. Erchless was put up for sale in 2018, after eighty-three years in the Phipps family.

West of Westbury High School, more of the semi-rural feel of Old Westbury. A glimpse of Westbury House is visible in the upper right of the photograph.

The Joshua Titus house on Post Road in Old Westbury, built *circa* 1750, is seen in a *circa*-1870s photograph. There are still several eighteenth- and early-nineteenth-century buildings left in Old Westbury, but many have been razed over the last 100 years as the land was purchased from Quaker families and large mansions built.

Looking east along Jericho Turnpike from the pedestrian bridge that leads to Westbury High School. In 1904, this stretch of roadway was the site of the grandstand for the first-ever Vanderbilt Cup Race. A historic marker on the south side of Jericho marks the historic moment.

The buildings of Hicks Nurseries are visible in this photograph looking north from the Drexel Avenue School. The school property and the homes in this image were all once part of the Hicks Nurseries property before some of the land was sold off.

OPPOSITE PAGE:

This image pair shows the narrow strip of Westbury proper that lies between Jericho Turnpike and the Northern State Parkway just north of Carle Place High School. The most notable structure in this neighborhood is the nineteenth-century mansion that is now called Westbury Manor, which was originally located on the north side of Jericho Turnpike. The second image captures the Northern State just before its sudden jag to the north at the westernmost limits of Westbury. The entirety of the land between Carle Road, Jericho Turnpike, and the Northern State Parkway was owned by just eight property owners as late as 1939.

When the Northern State Parkway was built in the 1930s, it literally cut through Westbury, taking land and separating the northernmost parts from the rest. Try to imagine what Westbury looked like before it was sliced open (and stitched back up through the construction of several bridges connecting parts north with the rest of Westbury).

This vintage 1930 aerial photograph looks south from just north of where the Northern State now cuts through Westbury. What is notable here is the large swath of property owned by the Hicks family nursery business.

Hicks workers in a *circa*-1910 photograph. Back then, as is true now, Hicks required numerous workers to keep it running smoothly. The big customers in those days were estate owners who often wanted to buy fully grown trees and have them planted on their Gold Coast properties.

OPPOSITE PAGE:

Above: The Van Velsor House originally stood on the east side of Post Avenue at the current site of the Northern State Parkway and was moved when the highway was built to Oxford St, where it stood at least until the 1970s.

Below: The area where the Westbury Middle School is located was once called Westbury Terrace. A large piece of the land north of what is now the Northern State and south of Jericho Turnpike was owned by Samuel Adams Warner Baltazzi (1878-1959) in the early twentieth century. Baltazzi was the grandson of New York architect Samuel Adams Warner, and was a sportsman and Democratic candidate for Congress in 1920. The property was still in the Baltazzi family as of 1939, after the Northern State was built.

With the construction of the Northern State Parkway, exit 32 offered direct access to Post Avenue, which runs through the heart of Westbury. Travel time to Westbury from many locales both east and west was drastically reduced.

Trees on either side of the Northern State Parkway create a semi-rural feel as you approach Westbury from the west. The image at top is looking east from Ellison Avenue and at bottom, from the Hicks "Dirt Road" bridge.

By the time you get to Fulton Street, approaching the Post Avenue exit, there's finally a sign of civilization. What would this part of Westbury look like today if the highway didn't come through?

The homes in the section between the Northern State and Jericho Turnpike west of Post Avenue and east of Woods Road are an eclectic mix of styles and ages. For example, the first four homes on Park Avenue east of the Fulton Street bridge, were built in 1927, 1913, 1991, and 1989, respectively.

The wooden school that used to be located near the current middle school was built in 1895 and stood until 1935.

This brick school building, which was located just off Post Avenue not far from the wooden school building, was built in 1909 to accommodate students from kindergarten through third grade.

The oldest building in the Westbury Middle School complex was originally the first Westbury High School (built 1924) before the high school moved across Jericho Turnpike to its current location.

The middle school complex as seen from the southeast. In the faint distance are the skyscrapers of Midtown Manhattan, almost the exact same latitude as Westbury, which is literally a straight shot to the city.

The middle school property seen from the west. This image shows just how large the property is, a function of how long ago the property was acquired, at a time when large parcels of land were available.

This image is a reminder of how much change the highway brought to Westbury. Construction was not just limited to the main highway right-of-way, but at Post Avenue involved the on and off ramps for exit 32.

The Westbury Library, though a fine library, is remarkable not in and of itself but mainly for the separate Children's Library building (top of photo), which was built in 1924 and was one of the first children's libraries in the entire country. It was funded by the widow of Robert Bacon, former Secretary of State under President Theodore Roosevelt and one of the most distinguished citizens in Westbury's history.

195
HOME
INNING
GUEST
BALL
STRIKE
OUT
H
E

Looking north northeast from Jefferson Street toward Cambridge Avenue. Note that here the Northern State is carried by a bridge over Cambridge, whereas to the west, the rest of the Westbury bridges carried local roads over a depressed Northern State Parkway. To the north, beyond, are the hills of Old Westbury and Brookville.

OPPOSITE PAGE:

Above: A view of the Rockland Street side of the library. At right is School Street, aptly named not just because of the middle school, but because the earliest Westbury village school was built on the corner *circa* 1840. The building, though since modified, still stands today and is noted by a historical marker on the spot.

Below: The Westbury Recreation Department is housed in a former Colonial-style residence at 357 Rockland Street, that dates to 1906.

Looking east and southeast from Cambridge between Rockland and Jefferson. These streets were nonexistent in 1906, at which time there were but a few owners of all the land visible in these images, but by 1914 the properties had been sold and the land subdivided and streets laid out. This coincides with the big building boom in Westbury as more estate workers needed homes near their places of work.

Oxford Street *circa* 1912-14, around the time when homes were first being built in this neighborhood.

The west side of Post Avenue between the Northern State and Lewis Avenue has changed dramatically since the early twentieth century, perhaps more so than any other stretch of Westbury's main street.

This image pair shows McCarthy's Store on Post Avenue, which would later become Kraemer & Mulligan Law Office, 432 Post Avenue. Seen around the turn of the twentieth century and again in 2006, the building was demolished a few years before the publication of this book.

The Westbury United Methodist Church was built in 1949 on a narrow strip of land on the eastern end of Asbury Avenue, between Fulton Street and Post Avenue.

The current Methodist church replaced an earlier building that used to stand at Belmont Avenue and Fulton Street.

The office building parking lot at Fulton and Belmont is where the Methodist Church once stood. The office building (265 Post Avenue) was built in 1985.

Much of the land on the west side of Post Avenue in the foreground of the view seen here (looking south down Post Avenue) was formerly part of the Wilbur Lewis farm. The old nineteenth-century farmhouse stood until the turn of the twenty-first century before it was replaced by the Titus Lewis Windhorst apartment complex at bottom center of the photo, and the home just north of it. Herman Windhorst was the name of the owner of the property in the 1920s.

In the 1920s, before the Northern State, Asbury Avenue (at right) was just another street like those to its south and parallel (Castle, Liberty, etc.), and it only ran from Post Avenue to the Hicks property. At that time there were two more streets laid out north of and parallel to Asbury Avenue, which were destroyed when the highway was built.

A walking and bicycle path winds around the Drexel Avenue School property which used to be part of the massive Hicks Nurseries land ownings, until the mid-twentieth century. I have often wondered which of the old trees on the property are from the Hicks era.

Looking west toward the Lewis Avenue dead end and the Drexel School property. In the distance, the 342-foot-high North Shore Towers in Queens are visible.

Opposite page:

Above: The Drexel Avenue School was built in 1952 in response to a growing population.

Below: Lewis Avenue's dead-end (center) dates back to when the street was first laid out in the first decade of the twentieth century and it stopped suddenly at the Hicks Nurseries property. After the Hicks land was sold, the dead end was preserved with same boundary due to the construction of the elementary school.

The bulk of the homes in the West Village section were built between 1905 and 1930, with a big building boom coming in the teens as more and more Gold Coast estate workers looked to build in Westbury.

A similar view of the Lewis Avenue area in 1912 captures the area under development.

Post Avenue was a direct line to many of the large estates to the north. North of Jericho Turnpike, Post led right into the land of Gold Coast mansions, with connections to other Old Westbury and Brookville roads. Estate owners could find all kinds of supplies in Westbury Village, which was the nearest village of any notable size.

The homes closest to Post Avenue were the first to be built, as proximity to Post was desirable.

Looking southeast from the Recreation Center baseball field toward Westbury South and New Cassel. Two skyline landmarks are the Westbury Water Tower and the Nassau University Medical Center.

Looking due north from Belmont Avenue. The site of the apartment complex on the corner of Lewis Avenue and Post Avenue was formerly occupied by an early-twentieth-century building that in its final iteration housed a television repair shop on the ground floor and apartments on the second floor.

A red box from the Red Box gift shop that once occupied the building at 289 Post Avenue (now an apartment complex).

The Space opened in 2014 to much local fanfare. It was a triumphant return of a blighted movie theater that had been closed for several years and had an uncertain future. The renovated and refurbished building is home to concerts and private events, and has featured such impressive big-name acts as Billy Idol, Art Garfunkel, and America.

The Westbury Theater building as it appeared several years before it was renovated.

Many of the buildings on Post Avenue were the beneficiaries of a grant for a façade improvement program around 2004. A similar facade improvement incentive program was launched again in 2018.

The James Seaman house seen around the turn of the twentieth century. It was originally located east of School Street on the north side of Cross Street. When the dairy farm was sold it was moved to south of Cross Street. The Seaman farm extended from Cross Street to north of Rockland and included the land that the library is on.

Looking from Carle Place High School to the east, Westbury limits begin at Carle Road. Development happened fast here, as in much of Westbury. As of 1906, the land in the foreground was owned by solely Anna Willets, Benjamin Post, and Harry Feltman. By 1914, the streets in the Westbury Gardens section as it was then called (Magnolia, Webster, etc. and south), had been laid out.

There was once a water tower on Drexel Avenue, dating back to the early twentieth century. The photographs on pages xx and x were taken from the top of that water tower.

The Westbury Water Park, formerly site of the water tower, is where fireworks are set off during the annual St. Brigid feasts in June and August. The Water Park was part of the Hicks Nurseries property, which extended all the way to Maple Avenue as late as the 1920s.

The homes north of Drexel Avenue between Ellison Avenue and Plainfield Street date to the mid-twentieth century or later, built on property owned for nearly 100 years by the Hicks family, who needed a lot of property in order to grow hundreds of trees for their customers.

Opposite page:

Above: Lascelle Hardware at 229 Post Avenue (at Winthrop Avenue) in 1922, with William Conklin behind the counter.

Below: Lascelle's sold electric appliances, among other items. This image, also from 1922, shows George Lascelle behind the desk.

TEMP-RITE

DIM-A-LITE
SAVES CURRENT

The Village Hall on Linden Place. The incorporated Village of Westbury dates back to 1932. Until Old Westbury incorporated in 1924, Westbury and Old Westbury were one entity.

Opposite page:

Above: Looking south from north of the Northern State in 1951, Carle Road is on the right and Ellison Avenue at left. The section of newly built houses in this image is easily identifiable by the lack of trees.

Below: This view was taken from the Drexel Avenue Water Tower *circa* 1910-12. Grand Street is in the foreground and Maple Avenue runs across the center of the image.

Bird's-eye View of Westbury, N. Y.
4031

Looking west from Fulton and Belmont Streets at the vintage 1910s and 1920s colonial homes.

The three-story tan brick Deferrari Building is one of the oldest surviving structures on Post Avenue. It once housed an Atlantic & Pacific store, the ancestor of the modern A&P supermarkets.

This image, looking west from behind Rite Aid, shows the back of the beautiful Westbury firehouse, located on Maple Avenue. The building was authorized in 1929 and completed in 1932.

The front of the Westbury Firehouse can be seen in this view, as well as a recently built apartment complex. Several apartment complexes have been built in Westbury in the last twenty years, helping create much needed affordable housing to entice young Long Islanders to stay on the island.

When they were built, the vintage Westbury 1900-1930 homes like this one on Morgan Place, were all sided with wood. The vast majority of the remaining old homes have since been re-sided with vinyl or other materials.

The St. Brigid/Our Lady of Hope Regional School opened on Maple Avenue (on land purchased from the Hicks family in 1947) in 1955, moving from smaller quarters on Post Avenue. Over 1,000 students were enrolled in the first year; by the 1960s, at its peak there were 1,600 students there.

The building in the foreground was formerly a convent (built 1965) housing the School Sisters of Notre Dame, replacing a smaller building on Post Avenue. The number of nuns teaching in Catholic schools declined over the years and the building was no longer needed. As of 2019, it is the Westbrook Preparatory School.

Looking north along a snowy Post Avenue in 1934. As of 2019, the Nassau County Republican headquarters is housed in what used to be a bank, and the Punta Cana Restaurant (formerly Maria's Bakery) is in the location that used to be the post office.

The Westbury Village Piazza under construction in 2007. It was built on the former site of a gas station, and during the early twentieth century was the home of the Harris family, which was moved to Fulton and Wilson Streets. As of 1906, the Westbury Hook and Ladder Company was housed in a building roughly at the northern edge of today's Piazza.

Since its completion, the centrally located piazza has become a place for concerts, film showings, and a weekly summertime farmer's market. At left is Benny's Ristorante (seen a few months before it closed), housed in a historic old building that has anchored the corner of Post and Maple Avenues for over 100 years.

The heart of Westbury Village, the main stretch of Post Avenue, features numerous restaurants and various shopping options, including a large Rite Aid drugstore which opened in 1998 on the site of what was once a supermarket.

Old medicine bottles rescued from Barley's Pharmacy (closed 1998), which was for decades a fixture on Post Avenue at Butler Street. As of 2019 the space is occupied by Maria's Bakery, after a brief stint as an antique store.

The stretch of Post Avenue between Maple Avenue and Orchard Street features some vintage buildings, including the old Barley's Pharmacy building at the corner of Butler and Post.

Old mixes with new all along Post Avenue—the three-story 2010s building that as of 2019 houses a discount store is next to and across the street from early-twentieth-century buildings.

Butler Street at Post Avenue around the turn of the twentieth century. Note that Post is a dirt road.

The Long Island Rail Road's Westbury station building, located on the south side of Union Avenue, has changed a lot over the years. Westbury's growth during the mid- to late-nineteenth century is due in part to its accessibility by railroad, being on the main line.

Union Avenue was inundated during a major flood in 1918. It was such a dramatic event that postcards such as this one showing the disaster were actually made and sold.

The Breezy Hill section of Westbury is located south of the railroad tracks and west of Post Avenue. Many Italian immigrant families from the town of Durazzano settled in this section, near St. Brigid's Church.

St. Brigid's Church on Post Avenue was one of the first Catholic churches in what is now Nassau County. The current building is the third one to stand on the spot. Its immediate predecessor was moved across the street and is now St. Anthony's Parish Hall.

First Communicants lined up in front of St. Brigid's Church in May 1959.

Opposite page:

The Holy Rood Cemetery, seen here from across Post Avenue at top and from Dryden Street at bottom, is a 65-acre Catholic cemetery that incorporates the earlier burial grounds of the original St. Brigid's Church.

Among the famous burials at Holy Rood are the "Unsinkable" Molly Brown (*Titanic* survivor), former CIA Director William Casey, and novelist Ayn Rand. Molly Brown's stone is just right of the pathway leading to the Post Avenue gate in the image at bottom.

The corner of Union Avenue and Post Avenue was the site of Luessen's Hotel, built 1900, which later became Nino's and then Piping Rock Restaurant. The building suffered a massive fire in 1999 and was not salvaged. The Horizon Apartment complex is now on the site.

Until a bridge was built in 1914, the LIRR crossing at Post Avenue was at grade. This site was the location of the country's first ever train-automobile collision, in 1901, when an auto racer visiting from France had his car smashed by an oncoming train. The 100-year-old bridge was recently replaced.

Above and opposite page: The Westbury Coal Yard, managed by Charles Levi, was located about where the Bristal Assisted Living Facility stands today. The 140-suite Bristal opened in 2002.

WESTBURY
COAL YARD
CHAS LEVI MANAGER.
I. HICKS PROP.
HOWE
SCALE.

In this view looking east from along Union Avenue, old and new buildings are both visible. Newest in this image is the storage facility on the south side of the tracks. Some of the Union Avenue buildings are quite vintage; Bartlett Tree Experts is housed in the two-story white structure (at bottom right) that dates to 1900.

OPPOSITE PAGE:

Above: Looking east towards the Westbury community of New Cassel. Originally settled by former German Revolutionary War soldiers, New Cassel was also home to pioneering African-American families.

Below: The African Methodist Episcopal (AME) Zion Church is a historic structure and its cemetery has burials of some well-known nineteenth century African-American families in the area, including names such as Levi and Bunn.

A train heads east on the mainline tracks past the School Street at-grade crossing. The horns of passing trains can be heard in much of Westbury, and even the rumble of the trains themselves, on a clear night. This crossing was where a tragic train-car accident occurred in early 2019, killing three people.

The Dryden Street School, just south of the railroad tracks and east of School Street, was built in 1952, another response to the post-war baby boom that hit the nation.

Warehouses along Dickens Street just south of the LIRR tracks. The building at left dates to 1951.

A heavily industrial section of Westbury lies in the triangle south of Union Avenue between the railroad tracks and Grand Boulevard. Some of these warehouse buildings date to the 1950s.

As of 1927, the entire area south of the railroad tracks to Old Country Road, between School Street and Grand Boulevard, was owned by someone named Cantor with no streets laid out yet.

The one-million-gallon Westbury Water Tower was erected in 1947. The earlier water tower off Drexel Avenue only had a capacity of 100,000 gallons.

Looking toward what was called the Morningside Heights section of Westbury. This area used to be directly across Old Country Road from Roosevelt flying field, and is now in close proximity to major shopping centers.

Looking south from the Charles J. Fuschillo Park in Carle Place toward the shopping along Old Country Road. Despite it being the location of Lindbergh's take-off, the most famous flight in aviation history outside of Kitty Hawk, nothing was done to save even a small part of Roosevelt Field from destruction.

This area of Westbury south of the train tracks and just east of Carle Road, was entirely undeveloped as of 1914, but by 1927 streets had been laid out.

The Westbury border with its western neighbor Carle Place is irregular and thus very fluid. Many Westbury residents eat or shop there on a regular basis. This image shows the Carle Place Station, for Westbury commuters the last stop before their home station. Our Lady of Hope Church is visible at center.

The Covanta waste-to-energy plant (opened 1989) at 600 Merchants Concourse is one of the tallest structures on all of Long Island, with a smokestack that rises 382 feet high and can be seen from miles away.

A home on Manhattan Avenue, just off Old Country Road, seen in a 1955 photo. Most of these houses just off Old County Road were small, enlarged over the years.

Southern Westbury from Carle Road. Landmarks on the horizon from left to right include the Westbury water tower, the steeple of St. Brigid's Church, Nassau University Medical Center, Covanta Energy smokestack, and the Carle Place water tower.

This 1936 aerial shows the newly completed Roosevelt Raceway in the foreground, and the Salisbury Golf Course across Merrick Avenue from the race track, which would later become part of Eisenhower Park. Further north is Old Country Road and St. Brigid's Church is visible along Post Avenue (aka Merrick south of Old Country).

This colorful program is from the 1936 George Vanderbilt Cup Race, a direct descendant of the Vanderbilt Cup Races held by William K. Vanderbilt in the early years of the twentieth century on local roads in Westbury and adjacent villages.

Roosevelt Raceway enjoyed decades of prosperity before it closed in 1988. The area, seen in this view, was eventually developed into retail and housing.

Looking west from roughly the spot where Charles Lindbergh's plane, The Spirit of St. Louis, took off the morning of May 20, 1927. Back then much of what is in this image was part of Roosevelt Field—the airport.

Avalon Westbury, with 396 homes, was opened in 2006 as Archstone. All residents were evacuated due to an epidemic of black mold found in the buildings, but the problem was later resolved and the complex reopened.

Opposite page:

Above: Looking north from the Source Mall parking lot toward the residential neighborhoods north of Old Country Road.

Below: It's amazing how much of what was once the flat runways of Roosevelt Field are now the flat parking lots of all the retail that replaced the airport.

The southern part of Westbury was once part of the great expanse of the Hempstead Plains. This *circa*-1910 image taken from west of what is now Merrick Avenue shows what the area used to look like.

OPPOSITE PAGE:

Above: Looking at Stewart Avenue from the entrance to Eisenhower Park. North and south of Stewart Avenue here were once part of the Meadowbrook Club. The upper right side of the image is now mainly commercial, developed after 1950 and the closure of the club along with the closure of Roosevelt Field, and further developed with the closure of Roosevelt Raceway decades later.

Below: Eisenhower Park was formerly the Salisbury Club, an exclusive golf club owned by Joseph Lannin, owner of the Boston Red Sox who traded Babe Ruth to the Yankees (and also owner of Roosevelt Field). The Westbury Water tower is visible to the north.

1600 Stewart Avenue stands where during the late nineteenth through mid-twentieth centuries, the famous Meadowbrook Club was located. As late as 1939, this hunting and sporting club owned all the land from Stewart Avenue south to Hempstead Turnpike, between Merrick Avenue to further west than where Merchants Concourse/Endo Boulevard is currently located.

OPPOSITE PAGE:

The only thing that hasn't changed in the last 100 years in this area south of Old Country Road—there has continuously been a golf course in this location since the 1910s.

Program from the 1960 Vanderbilt Cup Race held at Westbury.